sweet husk

sweet husk

CORRIE WILLIAMSON

PERUGIA PRESS
FLORENCE, MASSACHUSETTS
2014

Perugia Press extends deeply felt thanks to the many individuals whose generosity made the publication of *Sweet Husk* possible. Perugia Press is a tax-exempt, nonprofit 501(c)(3) corporation publishing first and second books of poetry by women. To make a tax-deductible donation, please contact us directly or visit our Web site.

Book Design by Susan Kan, Jeff Potter, and Corrie Williamson.

Cover art is *Mystery of Chaco Canyon, Summer/Winter Solstice*, mixed media on raw burlap, diptych, 48" x 78" each panel, by Martha K. Iwaski (1934–2013). Used with permission of the owner, Pamela Burnham, with gratitude to Eric Swanson Photography.

Author photograph by Kate Thompson/Betty Clicker Photography.

Grateful acknowledgement is made for excerpts from:
Wendell Berry, "Damage" from *What Are People For? Essays* © 1990, 2010 by Wendell Berry. Reprinted by permission of Counterpoint Press.
Hildegard of Bingen, "Antiphon for Divine Wisdom" from *Symphonia: A Critical Edition of the Symphonia Armonie Celestium Revelationum*, edited and translated by Barbara Newman © 1988. Reprinted by permission of Cornell University Press. All rights reserved.
Deborah Digges, "The Way Into Stone" from *Rough Music* © 1995 by Deborah Digges. Reprinted by permission of Alfred A. Knopf.
Seamus Heaney's *Beowulf: A New Verse Translation* © 1999. Reprinted by permission of W. W. Norton & Company, Inc.
Homer, *The Iliad*, translated by Stanley Lombardo © 1997. Reprinted by permission of Hackett Publishing Company.
James Wright, "March" from *The Collected Poems* © 1961 by James Wright. Reprinted by permission of Wesleyan University Press.

Library of Congress Cataloging-in-Publication Data
Williamson, Corrie.
 [Poems. Selections]
Sweet husk / Corrie Williamson.
   pages cm
Includes bibliographical references.
ISBN 978-0-9794582-7-9
I. Title.
PS3623.I5673A6 2014
811'.6--dc23

                             2014009782

Perugia Press
P. O. Box 60364
Florence, MA 01062
info@perugiapress.com
www.perugiapress.com

For my parents, John and Marilee

Contents

Has this fellow no feeling of his business, that he sings at grave-making?
—*Hamlet*

Remains

Anatomists and archaeologists call them
disarticulated bones, as if the scattering

of our bodies made us voiceless. As if
dead but whole we might still speak.

◆

We waited through fall and into winter,
but you were silent, ribs clasped to spine,

jaw firm, talus and tarsus intact:
the body's perfect alphabet beneath the snow.

◆

When the farmer inspecting his fenceline
found your bones in the grass

they were startling as sycamores
among oaks and pines. Just as speechless.

◆

They'll put you in the ground now, say
that you're home, hope you'll answer

each question that remains. The rest of us
will wish away the season, watch crocuses

come up. Wait for summer nights to cool, and
walk among the ridges, rattling our speaking bones.

one

The Evolution of Nightmare

With hair bound up, she unburdened herself
Of her worst fears, a wild litany
Of nightmare and lament . . .
                    Heaven swallowed the smoke.
                                    —Beowulf

In the dream, the linguist
with flaming scalp explains
how the language we speak
and all its sisters
trace back to their mother
tongue through a common word

for *honey*—our lexicon lapping
at an old, ambrosial root.
Yes, I say, but what was Grendel's
skin like? We know him
through that one word: *gæst*,
but if he bristled with fur

pearled with moor-frost or yearly
sloughed a scaled hide,
time does not reveal. Now
the old poet in whiskey tones
takes the chalk and tells
how the dead wear our clothes

and slip through
the sod. So perhaps he wore
the earth like a coat?
The most ancient known
word for man means

of the earth. Adam means *red.*

Now it is my mother speaking,
only she stands at the kitchen
window washing glasses,
the Revere Ware
a glinting sky of copper
moons, near the Revelation

that hung there always: *Behold,*
I stand at the door and knock . . .
I ask her, *but what about*
the monsters? Her reply
is in no language but she sings
a high, clear note that swims

like mercury minnows
in my blood. I take a dishtowel,
whisper into her hair,
Mama, how to tell the guest
from the ghost
wearing the same sweet husk.

The Mole, the Sweet Potato, and the Possibility of Allegory

On the table, a heap of sweet
potatoes, holes chewed
through the skin of some.

Wedge of orange meat
where a mole encountered
it underground: star-flesh

at the end of his nose bumping
straight into the subterranean
mother lode, blindly caressing

the tuber with the branched
mitts of his hands, scenting out
its complicated rough contours,

dusky odor of the roots'
snarl, gnawing into the soft
fibers which he can't know

are the shade of a harvest moon
low on the horizon. He eats
awed, but when he leads

the other moles here to share
the gift, line of them shuffling
in the tunnel, vein teeming with dark

blood toward a heart, there is only
an empty socket, a room whose walls
are soil, faintly fragrant.

My Father, Digging

My father writes to tell me he's dug another grave—
a farm animal gone down: old goat, friend of mine
from childhood days in the tall grass. He gives
those bones to the March ground, where the moon

frosts the earth at night, and the sun bleaches dry
what stays above ground. Hard enough, that winter soil,
to make a man sweat in the rough light of late day,
set his shovel in a clod, and look out over the still

afternoon, the hard slice of the gully, the hills lifting
and lowering cedars. Over the years he's slit the dirt
many times with a spade, in every season, red clay lofting
over his shoulder, opening wider the earth's dark draft.

Where the Sentence Ends the Sentiment Burgeons

Years since the old woman's grandson turned
early to ash and years since she's seen the young
woman who was his lover but seeing her now
extends her arms crying you look just the same
as that first day coming up the driveway I saw you
forking hay from a feedtrough as the chaff
drifted in the sun and in the long wild loops
of your hair waving and laughing as if I knew you
already and him leaning on the pitchfork and smiling
the black seed of his dying already planted between
his hips brittle and black as a walnut smiling
as if he'd live forever or perhaps as if he knew
but it was all right because that night he would lie
by the young woman below the grandparents'
bedroom with the windows wide and know the yard
gonged with the deep blue temple bells of hyacinth
that the cows sucked moisture from the dark and the owl
in the barn laid her eggs slowly through the night's
course so that the hatchlings would feed
on one another and the girl's hair was a great
mystery flowing over him to mix with his
young man's beard red as falu paint on a Swedish
cottage or red as the tongue of the bowsprit
his brother will invoke not long from now wishing
to launch the body out to sea burning and red
as the ruff of twin foxes who bark and snarl
chasing each other through alfalfa rows until
they both roll showing the golden scythe
of their bellies to the moon and she shows them hers.

Scala Naturae, or Southern Vivisection

Science, we learned, was a linear endeavor. I chanted
King Phillip Came Over From Greece
Singing, my tongue carving

down the mnemonic, the stacked
taxa from Kingdom to my own *sapiens*
sapiens, the highest of whom,

lanky Mr. McLachlan, directed us
to take out the scalpel and climb
the ladder back up: first the worm in its grooved

and gutted sleeve, then the grasshopper,
unfolding layered wings, the teasing
needle to separate tangled ganglia

(mystery of song unexplained that day).
Onto the crawfish! The yellow
perch, the frog, and you may believe

whatever you please about man's
ascent, but take up those forceps and pry
open the scented pink envelope

of pigflesh. The deeper we'd go, the less
the thing became itself. This was
not in the dissection guide. Still,

the more complex the creature, the greater the fear
as one ascended the final stretch: the cat
laid across the resin-topped tables,

slight the chance, but paralyzing,
that the slit in the soft hide
would part unto a chain of kittens,

swabs of life put aside. *I will give you*
the treasures of darkness.
Old Mac at the blackboard, wearing his hand

over his thin white bones,
writing the nomenclature, the skeletal systems,
didn't hear the voice beneath

the scratch of chalk, hissing
Climb up, climb up, but I did, sitting pinned
to my chair, wondering when it would call me by name.

Plath's Bees

Did Sylvia tell the bees
when Otto passed,
as custom demands,
and as he surely would
have wanted? Perhaps
she sought them out
one by one in the fields
and garden, quivering
over thick barbs of
pink thistle or slipping
from a poppy's mouth.
Having abandoned
the veil and moon suit
perhaps she came
smokeless at dusk,
all but a few zealous
workers tucked in the hive,
and she told them, voice
soft with the messenger's
humility, *I ordered this,*
clean wood box, her hair
falling over the slender
crack of the hive's
entrance, the last bees
crossing gently through it,
leaving yellow flares
of pollen there, as some
untamed sweetness
welled in her who knew
all along the Lord
was a beekeeper.

A Study of the Anthropologist: I

He said: Containment
is the child in the womb
and the corpse in the ground. He said,
your luminous body will

combust automatically. The earth-diver
descends to the ocean bottom,
brings up land, and thus: creation.
At some point every great story presents

a holographic picture of itself. Digression
is the soul of anthropology
he said: the Inuit have three ways
to kill a wolf, and here's the second.

Take a strip of blubber and inside,
at a slight angle, embed and freeze
a knife blade. The hungry wolf
will lick and lick and lick

until it tastes salt. Not recognizing
the salt as the blood
from its own shredded tongue, the wolf
licks until he bleeds to death.

The soul through the mouth, after all.

The Whaler to His Wife

For many months I have slit
open the sea's belly, pulled from inside
her storm-skinned children
and opened them too. I peeled dark
into dark, a new skin within each,
as if a thousand fishes lived in one.

We each have a churning heart, and a song
under our bones. I've cut many out; still
I heard your sleep-sounds
pounding the deck, wrapped in the blood-soaked
skeins of harpoon lines, whipping back to me
down that taut, traveling length.

I come to you with oil burning,
have laid my boots
with their crust of gore
upon the stoop.

Your body, too, is sleek as wind.
Take me into your earthbound bed.
I have not forgotten
the glory of morning-cold blankets—
the stillness of your body
still tight inside them.

The Seed Jar

A camellia, you tell me,
when I ask what it is,
the white blaze

that you've put in my hand,
bright faced in the dark.
A confused camellia, I say,

because October is sliding
into November, because the cold
comes up from the stones under my feet

and the wind tosses
the bushes in your yard,
because already

the blossom in my hand shakes.
But no, you're saying, this is their season,
appearing right on time, and you show me

how it is double-flowered,
a healthy froth. Brave, to bloom
under these cold constellations,

into this unforgiving weather,
where the night slips through the chinks
in your cabin walls, bound in wood braid,

where our skin becomes
translucent against the wind,
a mica sheen upon the body,

where you offer a name
to everything that grows and declines:
the fallen cherry you used

to whittle a spoon, the black locust,
which you covet for firewood,
because it burns so hot

and slow, is practically
good as coal. But what
of the unnamable inside us,

brittle and burning in the body's jar,
neither anthracite nor isinglass,
beneath that tiny mouth, ready

to be cracked, to be broken and
spilled out, where it must seek the soil,
be buried and take root, or die.

two

Ruin Song

Chaco Canyon, New Mexico

I have no gift for this waiting.
And yet I would be stone.
        —Deborah Digges

I.

If history begins with a house, it is a stucco bungalow
where the wash narrows and cliffs drop away,

bearing windows that watch the sun fragment
morning and evening around the banded butte.

Here the rangers came for dinner one
by lonely one. The first had slender hands and told

a story well: legend of the Yenaldooshi, shape-
changer, and the man who offended him, at whose

door one night a body hurled itself, shrieking
through the dark, throat full of wind and nettles,

clattering tooth and claw upon the window,
and in the morning: a wolf's skin upon the stoop.

I wash the dishes in cold water, toss
another mouse corpse in the garbage and tick

the mark of its death on the ledger. My hands
in the glinting sink are the pale bellies

of starfish. Body in its static skin,
its daily dress. Wet-palmed I go outside and press

them up against the sky, try to imagine
this place in its days as ocean. Can't. Unless

it is to lean on the porch's beam and look out

over pale desert grass, glittering with scorpions

taut and white as tendon, until the black ground
mirages to water, until the brows of the dead

begin to rise toward me from beneath, until
like reflection, they nearly touch the surface.

2.

Pots aren't people, we'd remind
one another, again and again, holding up
sherds to the stiff new sun, saying

　　　　　Mineral, organic, based on the way
the paint's edges blurred to nothing.
But what did we have?—not the wet
brush in our hand. Brightness

of the occasional rarity: a malachite
arrowhead the color of pine needles, the cold heft
　　　　　of an ax-head,

the turquoise bead I slipped in my pocket (thief!)—
leaf-shaped, its perfectly drilled hole
for suspending from a neck. It's everywhere,

　　　　　after all, the turquoise. Even the ants
covet it: root around in their hills
long enough, and tiny blue flakes
　　　　　　　　　sift up to the surface.

I dream the vengeance of the kingly dead:
dressed only in skeleton
and azure stone, come to my bed to lay

　　　　　the bare bones of his hand around my wrist,
a bracelet of distals

tightening. To buy time, I tell him how
I had missed the lunar eclipse

I waited hours to see. How it happened
below the horizon: a black bowl

set in a white bowl, set in the earth.

3.

Tell about the bones.

        Not enough, scholars have said. The earth having surrendered
too few from her churning. (And those dressed richly,

        weighted to the grave with ropes
of turquoise, black pots of maize, a bronze bell,
the jet frog that calls forth rain.)

        Abacus of bone that does not equal
metropolis: instead, they say,
        worshipping place of the honored dead.

        This is not what I believe.

They are everywhere
and unreachable. Not just the millennium dead, but the men
        who first disturbed them.

Tell about the bones.

        Pepper's? The young one, city-boy, trigger happy,
who perched on his cot in long underwear shooting
        at kangaroo rats in the tent, and once
            fired at a devil through the night, and found

at dawn the feathered mess of a great horned owl
shot off a ruin wall, the Navajo diggers whispering,
        refusing to touch a spade.

The bones: Wetherill's, old pot-scrounger, cliff-scaler, who pulled

thick vigas from the ceilings of the ruin to build
his house in its shade. What were you allowed
                    to keep? The first body the canyon took back
            in centuries, rippling russet over your bones
like the skin of a horse touched by the footstep
                    of a fly.

Tell a wishbone of rough juniper, sling-shotting
round stones from a dead river across the crack
            of the arroyo at the same damned stars.

4.

There is a payphone in the desert
from which I dial my mother. I do not say
this loneliness is an ocean, that it is miles
of dust before my words even cross a road
bearing a name. *Mother,* I say, *I climb*
the mesas, and on clear days can see
San Juan peaks to the north like a white
fish's spine. Mother, in the living heat
I sketch maps of absence. *Today,*
descending a rock shoot in the run-off's
worn path, what I believed were yucca needles
rose to my boot——a porcupine the size
of a dog, who showed me his arrowed teeth
and scaled the cliff. Mother, *the elk*
wear tracking collars. I do not
say, Mother, I am living in the valley
of the dead. Mother, at night the air-
conditioner shudders to a halt, the heater
stirs the blinds, clicking against window
glass. I swear he's there, coyote, the trickster,
the one who throws his voice between
canyon walls, ears laid back, his skittering
laugh: *What do you want with us? What*
could you possibly want?

5.

The sun writes an elegy at noon, cutting
the earth in two. Azimuth

      of rising, death the southern limit, seen
through parallax and refraction.

Chart the shadow patterns: iron
riddling the sandstone, the heat

      a spiral chipped into stone holds
through the day, the juniper cloven

toward the sun, the names
for the ruins pearls on the tongue:

      Bonito, Rinconada, Alto, Chetro
Ketl. Stars are only part

of the story, night's studded underbelly.
The shape of the crescent contains

      all endings. A dagger
through the heart of the season.

6.

Postcard to Edward Abbey in the afterlife:
Hardly an earnest desert, you'd say: scrubland and plateau,
summer rain riding in on wind sweeping the steppe's
wide floor.   But I've seen emptiness in the north:
eyes of raccoons in the treetops reflected in my headlamp
that long summer on the great lake dunes, their shape
in the mind an echo, a graph of perfect sleep rising
and falling between dream and darkness.   Here, tunnels
run in the earth, and ghosts rise up from the drum
to dance.   You swore there's no lack of water
in the desert, but just the right amount.   If hearth means
home, how many clustered sleep-bound around blue
embers, skin piñon-scented, fires a winking mirror
of the winter sky?   What's dangerous is beautiful, what's
beautiful, dangerous, and those who are sure
there's no heaven have spent more time imagining it
than those who believe with certainty it's up there.   Reply
post haste.   You had the need I have: for sense.
Like any remains, it may be buried, a crease within a fist,
vanishing into the ground or reappearing in flashes of blue,
unwhole, unsearchable as your stubborn heart under dust:
shriveled cob, black husked tongue.

7.

Cliff swallow,
gatherer of lost things
who knows
what can be built
from what

is found, flitting,
a quick breath
trembling the brush
beneath the sky's

bolt of unfurling
blue flannel, could
I give you, please,
the muscle
of my heart, lullabied

into the waterless sleep
of the desert,
to carry to your nest
and press among

the Mormon grass
and amaranth and clay,
a lining like frothed, rough
silk, which would wake
come spring
with the warmth

of the day and the young,
to thicken and pulse

around them
like the warning
beat of flood,
like moonlight, or news?

8.

I hunger for cold. Rest
in the shade of sandstone
etched with spirals and snakes.

The sky goes on and on
so I slit my eyes and think
of the arctic, of the bridge proposed

over the Bering Strait.
Why not? We'll cross
back: a chuffing herd of sedans,

fenders gleaming with evening
sun. We will not burn and eat
their bodies. We'll build

no houses with their bones.
For miles, a waning
eye of land closing behind us,

returning to winter,
having forgotten
our talismans. (They were

wizened, wordless, anyhow.)
The land wears her corset
of cement. Our pockets empty

of seeds, our fingers
freeze. All is unfamiliar,
following exhausted breath

back into the cold
dark, our stories written
on palimpsests of ice.

9.

Then it must end with the home
beneath the ground. This is a garden of bone,
this is a bracelet woven

(which some call a city).

South is the best direction: the gap, points
of entry.

Evidence of: the use of the land
                                                         the use of the stone

(whether it was meant to be seen).

The sandstone bricks once painted white, after all,
        gleaming stories rising from the desert like vertebrae,
mandibles found all around the canyon

        connect to physical/spiritual worlds.

What is necessary to know? What knowledge I have of this place I guard
like a catamount, snarling.   You will take away nothing.

        What thresholds were exceeded:

sacred in character, symbolically charged

                                                         as a navel—
        lunar

                The inner alcove altar, and cliff

emerge from the underworld above the valley
floor, down into the floodplain below,
stairs cut the cliff, the scorch marks:
                a lengthy occupation.

One thing is clear—it's this:
if there is a life
after this one, sweet
and hard
        as this one

            it is to know the others.

three

The Wisdom of Dormancy

To lose the scar of knowledge is to renew the wound.
—Wendell Berry

The trees raise battlements
of spartan color, day goes slender,
shadows setting their sharp ears to the ground.

In my bright kitchen I mix gin
and tonic with the mint I carried here
in a terra cotta pot from half a country away.

In the land of those roots, my family counted
the winter dead like candles: days,
news, hours, the rising sun

dressing the beeches beyond
the glass in slim bony light. We read aloud
to them, sang, still—the flicker.

He tears leaves between his teeth
and kisses my mouth as if
spring could live in the tongue, as if

loss were not a perennial that blooms
in December, and I might forget
the slow muscling of its roots

the way a tree along a fence line
forgets, grows, and seams
around the barbed wire's scar.

While Picking Berries, I Recall the Childhood
Practice of Tying Junebugs to Strings,
Swinging Them Overhead like Balloons

It's a fine confusion, the hand
deep among small fruit
          and brambles, closing
around shadowy bice-black
sheen, unsure in that moment
          if it will grasp the blackberry
or the Junebug poised to gnaw,
and perhaps it will be the insect
          popped between the teeth,
rattling down the throat, its riven shell
sparking in the belly, while the berry
          is what's tied to a length
of slim twine and which circles
above, dark gloss in the dusk,
          returning and returning
          to ask for release, but with the peace
of a thing come
          into this world with a spine
for a spine.

My Father's Pronunciation

Somewhere in the past, in the Bedford
hills, you left behind the old way of speaking—

or mostly did: a few words you kept
unthinkingly, and I crouched in their wake

like a child with a Ball jar capped with hole-
punched cloth, that I might close them up,

stow them by my bed at night, be lulled to sleep
by the rustle of their wings against the glass.

Most of all, I wanted to save the word *bury:*
how you'd speak it like it was written,

so that when you said, *We had to bury the old man
in winter, with the ground frozen,*

the word rhymed with *fury,* not with *tarry.*

The Language of Birds

I.
Years ago, crows tongues were cut, sliced down the middle,
        straight to that strange bone inside—in hopes
they might summon a few human words.

Think of all that's been spoken to you,
        though not in your language, though not that you
could even hear; and all
that you tried to make speak, which held its silence.

2.
Evenings, light rides out of the valley like a slow blue horse. I go out
        in the dark. There's a fearful thing
about the passage of autumn to winter. Though I can't call its name,
it knows mine, like a bird, always speaking,
        now and then understood.

3.
January's cold whiplash, and I'm stunned
        by ice on the James.
Only so many months ago, autumn sneaking in, I put in my kayak
at Narrow Passage, watched the rain come in
        behind me. It broke, and broke
warm, tapping the trees' reflection
        on the wide water. Ahead, the geese told one another
of my bright boat,
and took off, trailing white wakes in the river, a slow
        rising, a long arm gesturing.

4.
Death licks the road with his red tongue. His hands are small, gray

and nimble

      as a coon's cupped around a pale egg.
I want to hear the words nested in my belly, feel them flash
against my throat, I want
a bone in my tongue, to ask how much

      of the fear is still inside me, its rained-upon wings
folded tight in my ribcage.

A Sparrow's Life's as Sweet as Mine

Each year before the autumn fires
we'd climb the ladder's tin rungs
to the roof. My father tied thick chain
to a length of rope and fed it clanking
down the chimney. Most house fires,
he explained, come from build-up
in the flue, creosote and pine tar
slicked to the inner walls: a would-be
howling throat of flame.
We scraped the danger away
with iron links. I never feared a fire
would take our lives: unimaginable
our bodies outlasting this house,
impossible as the first hunt I was permitted
to come on (after years of leaving
talismans in his coat pockets: a silver
leaf, an unopened pinecone,
green seaglass) when I held the doe's
rear legs as he reached inside her,
his fist closing around the lungs
forcing her leftover breath into the air
as a cold gasped cloud. Those rooftop
mornings, perched above our beds,
we'd hear metal shouldering against
brick, sloughing soot. In lucky years
there would already be a deer
hung in the garage, her muscle
marbling to blue in the cold.
And we'd listen for the thrum
of wings, the sparrow navigating
past the chain and out of that puckered

black mouth, past our pale faces
and into the chilled air, wings soft
with ash, nest knocked free into the empty
space our fires would safely lick.

Tapetum Lucidum

for M, living off the grid

I let the dog out and he bolts, quivering
as if to throw the moonlight off his blackness.

I think of you in your house, which is not
what most would call a house, built

of salvaged windows, evergreen planks. The year
you lived in the District, you promised

your father to always leave a half tank
of gas in the car. He was not paranoid, but the fact

of the matter was that the cities would go first,
dissolving, digesting themselves, and he wanted you

able to reach land without stopping—as if *land*
could mean nothing but *home*, as if *home* is always

safe, a place from which sustenance blooms.
When you owned land at last, you swore

it spoke to you—warned you the night the tornado
hawed through high branches to inkblot the moon.

You called your dog in quick, and she came,
as mine does now, the porch light snared in his eyes.

You will know them by their bright tapestry:
pupils' shining distance gives shape of skull,

movement of eyeshine shows methods
of locomotion—bobbing, weaving, leaping.

Can the land tell its secrets to the body?
This year, hurtling over vast fields to your door,

the interstate lay furred with the carcasses
of coyotes. Armadillos burst like swollen fruit,

and the Rorschach smear of blood on asphalt
spread wide its ragged wings, its stray-wire heart.

Surely it is not the flesh that warns us
against damage, but is carved by it

as a tree must cant to the wind, and if not felled,
concede to bend its form, to alter the shape

and scope of its reach. And yet you're out
there, and perhaps your eyes shine in the dark,

recalling the trove of what
is needed: rifle, cedar, seed, spark.

Umbrage

for Deborah Digges

Certain spring days I can conjure you
hissing *stone, lilac, hive.* How the air

must have cracked open when you died,
your ready fists full of earth, and maybe

it was more than the morning sun
flushing the forsythia leaves that made

me shiver. And maybe not. I would
have been bent over a book of ruins:

To build is to dwell, you believed, though
it's never that simple. Lascaux,

Chauvet, those caves your mind
moved through like wind with their stacked

beasts: horses, lions, stranger and lost
things drawn atop each other, or a series

of heads, webs of legs—whether herd,
lineage, nightmare, you didn't say.

Two ways to make a handprint—
the prehistoric artist coats the palm

and finger undersides with ochre or burnt
bone, presses against stone: a positive

image. For the negative, the hand
is laid bare against the wall, pigment sprayed

around it like music from a reed,
the surrounding space flaring into portrait

of absence. I can't explain the wet
bitterness socked in my chest that I didn't

know of you when you lived. What
I would have done with the knowing

doesn't matter, but here's news you missed:
they're saying the beasts with many painted

limbs and heads would have changed
by torchlight, would, cast alternately

in flickering light and shadow, become
sequence, become motion, could have raised

and lowered a single strong neck, or
heaved through stillness and raced along the wall.

July, and I Urge My Roots to Grow

I.

July, and the mud daubers arrive as they do each summer,
their bodies like brown glass beads strung on a wire.
They build their earthen cells on my back porch, long flutes
of dirt that grip the walls. In each cell, one egg.
In each cell, a dozen paralyzed spiders.

I split a nest just to see, shower the ground with curled,
poisoned green bodies, with the mother wasp's long toil.

2.

July, and I am beginning to understand the danger
of Prufrock's peaches. I eat them, ripe after ripe, each bite
a *do I dare?* held in the caution of the tongue
on that furred skin, the awareness of teeth pulling away
the fruit, down to the rough-backed bristle of seed.

In summer's heat, the body, a peach, tears more easily,
the flesh an unwelcome armor—the flesh too many
closed shutters. Inside, that cold center we ache to touch.
The skin tightens, moistens, longs to shed its excess.
Every small wound lets it loose, splits
the soft whiteness into breathless lips.

3.

July, month of fire. Here is my advice: take the one
you love, find a place in the grass where coolness
curls up from the ground. Watch the sky-strewn lights
rising in the bright bowl of his iris. Watch them bloom,
drape the night with their splayed arms, disappear.

4.
July, and the raspberries grow thick: one in your hand
is like a wasp's hive, built in tiny cells around a sweet hollow.

In this shimmering fever, my mother looks like an angel
with her knot of still-dark hair lifted above her neck,
and the skin of her arms brown around the white map
Vitiligo has drawn on her hands, as if some pale hidden
skin fights to emerge, to be seen. My father, earth-diver
of origin myths, puts on a straw hat and an angry red skin.

He goes down, down through the water, down
through the red clay, until he finds the sweet earth.
He brings it up. He lullabies it into birthing.
He promises me blackberries in August.

In Every House the Same Blue Flame

Blood on the rug, the hardwood,
the white vinyl kitchen tile,
and I can hardly stand the gentleness

with which the dog lets me roll
him to his side, inspect his paws' webbing.
The age-old problem: his joy

is my joy, the jaunty steps, nose
raised to wind, bearing the cold
indoors on his coat into my hands

which stroke that black gloss, proud
of this life in which he is no longer beaten
with socks full of coins. Meanwhile

the yard draws up glass after rain
like spring crocuses. History's shrapnel—
ghosts of old inhabitants buried

with the crockery. My friend calls, my hands
full of stained towels, darkness now
in her time zone, recalls her high school job

at the carwash next to Oakey's
Funeral Home, where they burned the dead
on Tuesday mornings. The scent. The dog

is fine, patrolling the rooms without
a limp and licking the bright tiles
where I wiped away his blood.

A Study of the Anthropologist: II

At night in the tent. A warm
Yucatan breeze, a moment
alone. She turns on the tape-recorder.
His voice played back to her
is a bowl, is a vessel,
and she closes her eyes to discover
its shape. Tongue like a potter's wheel,
and every word clay spinning,
rising into form, whole
coalescing around hole. Even
the words to describe the words
are music: fricative, bilabial,
alveopalatal. She studies the way
they change, how they branch and morph
and if you blink there's only
the tongue in your mouth
to lead you back. The word
for *sing* is *K'ay* with a hard stop. The voice
says the moon and the sun
dance together in a line.
Apocalyptic palindrome, she thinks,
the nonsense and the fear. Bats a fly
from her damp cheek.

The Comte de Buffon Composes a Nasty Note to Thomas Jefferson Regarding His Recurring Nightmares of the American Moose

I can't sleep anymore, with that thing stalking my dreams,
bugling down the halls of slumber, scraping its massive rough
knees across the marble till it lurches upright, its skull hung
like a loose boulder in that rancid pelt, its antlers trailing flaming
chandeliers. A new world! There's no new in the world,
or didn't you know? Hunkered down in the dirt, singing hymns
to your vines, expecting the dark earth to raise its head to you,
let you stroke its ears, and call it tame. Damn you, forget what I said—
let your people be smooth, your ground unfrozen, your *Ursus* bigger
than all the cathedrals of Paris. A new world. I'm an old man,
and even when sleep comes past those thundering hooves, I wake
whimpering like a dog remembering an old beating, who calls up
from his dim memory the hand's bones hard on his frail hide.

George Catlin's *Buffalo Hunt, Chase*

They fly above their shadows.
Somehow not a single hoof

of buffalo or harrying horse strikes
bulging earth. They hover,

girdling that lonely mother of a summit
like fleecy moths. Even the injured beast

who bears his wound like a red standard
curls his halved foot to the sky's slashed breast.

Leaning in—the scene is small—the gaunt
bow's tension grips my neck. At last

I can put my finger on it, here, how ghosts
are made, quiet as an almost-

vanishing, as the guilty rush that anchors
us back against the precipice's ache.

Migraine/Ecotone

My head's a dry spell, a paper lantern
patched with iron. The four a.m. train

      bullies through town, and here's
what's unforgivable: the mystery of its freight,

that I choose not to know what passes through
this place, pulling north, south, steaming

in the cold night like the breath of animals
who don't look up to watch it pass.

      Last spring, coming down
out of the Chuskas to the Arizona border,

just short of where pine-needle floor
      gives way to red dust: a mountain lake
frozen solid, men in lawn chairs on its gleaming

surface beside bucket fires:
ice-fishing in the desert sun.

      Wearing the pain now like a second skin,
a coat of scales, I ache

after that cold core through gray light: division
as frozen, ragged tunnel through which to slip. How

      do we reach them, the places that mend us?

The wind gathers, leaves leaning

shadows over the windowpane. If

it would rain, I think, all pressure would ease,
pain edging into sleep, cold raindrops meeting

the soil of my fall garden, wetting the spinach
palms, the silver trembling lettuce, the flowers

      of the sugar snaps, white fisted and starry with frost.

four

Once, in College, My Father Played Horatio

Wasn't Denmark cold in the heart
of winter? Wasn't the wind northerly,

blowing across the country's coastal
porches from the open sea, carrying its whisper

of worlds of ice? But the gravediggers
sing so cheerfully, praise their profession,

and no one (not even Laertes, leaping
into the grave with his wrenching cry—*Hold*

off the earth awhile!) breathes a word
about how knit-tight the soil must have been,

how his sister's last bed could only be made
by carving out a chamber of frost

from the earth's frozen ventricles.
No one knew this better than my father

who arrived for the December funerals
of his own father, then his brother,

to find the undertaker beside an idling
backhoe, grave undug, mourners set to arrive,

sputtering, *Too cold,* useless as a spade
against granite, and my father swore

that man had buried his last

Williamson, though he knew this winter

burial was no choosing. No good
to ask the dying for further persistence,

or to hold off until spring thaw. What could
he do but pray against custom, hands

splintering in the patient cold,
that insistent monologue of bone.

Terra Firma

My garden won't last in this dry Arkansas dust,
though I water it anyway, hose arcing

in my hand, keeping up the tomatoes' swaying survival,
the lavender's sweating. Through the slow blinding

of afternoon, a thin muslin across the eyes, I look into
the kitchen window. That folded paper took me by surprise

earlier, falling from a favorite book. I stay out
until the undersides of the walnut's leaves stream gold,

and the cicadas trill and churn the dusk. They came
from the soil, hauling their heavy shrouds, and one followed me

into my house, dive-bombed the lamp, hissing bloom of light
I silenced with a shoe, pressing its body against the bulb.

It died with a racket—a rust-snarled door swinging.
When I come in dark has settled, and that slender

preserved page is where I left it, bearing its
cargo, the fresh-eyed photograph of a face

I cannot ask to tell me
what, in the end, the ground gives up.

Why the Photograph of George H. Pepper Sitting on a Viga in Pueblo Bonito Reading the Bible Haunts Me

Because in the midst of it
      he has forgotten
            the mystery: New York city

boy who cradled the name
      archaeologist to his chest
            without having seen the dull

bulbous birthing of a skull
      from the ground until
            this desert requited enough jaw

bones alone to build a small
      gazebo. Because the entirety
            of his afterlife may be here

contained: the grainy black
      and white glare off plaster walls,
            the journal entries calling his mount

Senior Burro, the lists of lengths—
      this femur bone, that stone cell's
            remaining wall. Because there is nothing

but the room, and even that
      is invisible below. Because he must
            have sat very still, except his feet blur

as if dancing. Because as he reads
      of creation, the earth sighs through

the sipapu from which the ruin-builders

slipped up from the underworld.
      Because the underworld
            permeates. If bushes burn on the page

beyond it the sun snags
      in the creosote—testament to worlds within
            worlds, and also

                  that there is only the one.

Bear Hunters at McAfee's Knob

It's hard to breathe
In a tight grave . . .
—James Wright

Days past Christmas
and the men
          lean into the truck's cold

tailgate tugging cigarettes
          from canvas pockets
and cock their heads for the mournful curl
of a bay. I've come

to view my home country
          from a high dish
of rock that juts like a slipped
disk off the A.T.'s immense spine.

She must have found shelter by now,
          I think, though breath and smoke
          mingle in the narrow air:
signal of permission

to seek her still, the season winnowing,
last days before they cannot uproot her
          from the den, thick

with her litter, cubs
          which will keep the guns off her
          come spring if they endure
her sleep, suckling at her dense warmth

or gnawing the peeled away pads of her feet.
       I nod to the men, remembering
the Wright poem in which the cubs fall

from her hair as she leaves the den, and she
does not know them
except as a promise,
       a blueprint made of darkness

and heat against her side,
       knows them
as she does the hills, the cracks and folds

       of a land that yearly
rebirths her. We listen for the hounds,
their braided voice, its song—
       We are beasts of our word.

A Study of the Anthropologist: III

He named his child the Waiwai word
for *fish basket*.
In the forest they laughed,
white teeth among the green,
said, in their tongue,
Don't look now, and warned
of the jaguar
that had taken a liking
to stalking the long shadow of his body.
Later, as he bathed in the river,
it came to the bank, stood watching.
Nothing like the world
he had come from, no zoo-cat.
Immense. Two pairs
of eyes in the jungle, two dark skins
gleaming with Amazon water,
the longest stare
he would ever know. He opened
his mouth with the soul leaping up,
and then it was gone.

Farther down the river
a woman sang among the rushes.

Xanthus, Achilles' Immortal Warhorse, Rodeos in Amarillo

> *Ah, why did we give you . . . to a mortal,*
> *while you are deathless and ageless?*
> *Was it so you could share men's pain?*
> *Nothing is more miserable than man*
> *of all that breathes and moves upon earth.*
> *—The Iliad, XVII*

It was meant to be a gift, though the gods
should know by now it never is: sick of it

themselves, grown fidgety, restless, meddlesome.
It was harder on me of course than Balius,

him having never known speech while I tongue
the narrow trough of my mouth and half

expect words to return. Where he is now
I don't know. After a time, we gave up being

untamable, and let ourselves be led, be put
to whatever tasks men could imagine. They call

this place *Texas,* hot enough for wandering
souls, where all of time stretches before me

as an endless tunnel of wind. The children wear
strange hats and their boots point like nettles

between fence boards. Men wish to be thrown, and,
understanding, I toss them, light as milkweed,

as burdock. But how tiring to make a living
from this act of riddance: spur in the side and belly

raw, summoning the body's rage, a strap of leather
and bone buckled and desperate for breaking.

Love Poem for Naming

Find the word for it. Nightly sound
of breath
       beside me. Call it a hand

run up and down a length
of taut-skinned tree bark,
       poplar, maybe.

Arrowed shape
the old shipmakers
       harvested for masts.

Or possibly call it the rustle in the dry
wheat that grew wild through
       our back field,

where I built nests when I was small
as I imagined the speechless animals
       did, flag leaves

brittle, shush-saying over my head.
Hidden there
       just long enough

for my mother to worry. Come to the porch,
dishtowel on her shoulder,
       casting

my name over the afternoon.
Keen and honest
       as the iron

bell in the garden. I would
explode from the chaff,
         grassy-haired,

a wild grouse. Most nights:
his back.
         The moon

turns its white face between the blinds.
If I woke him,
         demanded, *The moon,*

name it, would he say
a bowl of gold butter
         on our breakfast table?

The upended shell of earth's silver
turtle twin? No,
         I'd reply.

An ivory Viking longship, tipping
into black sea. Your shoulder
         blades'

parenthetical. No, this: your body
is the boat, its fine,
         slumbered rigging—

that drumming in the keel.

Reading Charles Wright in the Desert

In the field, I learn by trying
that a dry bone will stick to the tongue—a good way
to tell it from stone or wood, to cull the once-living
from the always-still.
Corn no longer grows in the canyon, though it's a pleasure
to shuck it on the porch, as the sky collects
and burns around the buttes, the color of cumin powder,
and imagine the rincons bristling with the shadows of stalks.

I read you against the loneliness of this place, to force
a collision of landscape, to bring near
your cedar boughs and cold Shenandoah moon.
What would you say to all this—that perhaps some places
press upon the body with the force of home, and some
just weigh on you? I imagine you walking eastward from Isleta,
a white arrowhead in your mouth, singing
Swing low among the ironwood.

Perhaps it's like this, you would say: God made us
with our hearts in the ground, and a stone
under our tongues. Toward the mesas, the rain casts
its columned threads in bundles to earth,
and the old windmills, last of their kind, catch and spin, tug
the sky to the dusting soil. Or, you would say, perhaps
it is like this: the cottonwoods turn up their palms in the breeze,
remembering the new green hearts they bore in the spring.

Migraine/Ecotone II

One wing soars in heaven
one wing sweeps the earth
and the third flies all around us.
    —Hildegard of Bingen

The pain may be caused by passing between
extremes of temperature.   Summer a catalogue

of dust, fingers raked through the fringes of impossible
lives, out of the heat of the sun by three,

        afternoon spread wide, acres of potential
ache.   On weekends the two hour drive

to the nearest Walmart, blinking in fluorescence
and air-conditioning, palming the sleek

firework of a pepper, cans of tomato sauce.
        Deep in the monastery, far from the bright

air that congregates in window corners
where sunlight, pain, and sound   blur, Hildegard

knew her aura to be god.   When I had my first
I was sure I was going blind.   Singing

helped her, praise of explosions in the mind,
the brain's vocal center flaring too, tearing

at the seal of pain's envelope.   We voyage farther
than groceries to the Hopi mesas for a kachina dance,

watch from the rooftops as thick dancers, spirits
come down from the peaks, turn and bend.

On another roof across the plaza, golden
eagles perch and shuffle, waiting years

for sacrifice, their turn to seek the divide,
spirit-carriers, tethered to satellite dishes.

This Rough Magic

Something to do with Prospero,
how his hair was white
as coconut meat, but he hated
coconuts, hated the island
because it was ripe
with those rough-shod
bristle-haired fruits,
and he couldn't stomach
their sweet shavings
on even a cupcake. I tumbled
from the dream, room
alight with the threads
of thunder's split
seams, the dog trembling
at my ankles, and grasped
for the thing which seemed
the stuff of verse,
though it was all spilt
milk and shipwreck,
dove back into sleep
through the lightning
to seek it out, believing
there'd be no other
poem, no more dreams:
this the final storm.

Leaning Toward Manifesto

Composting is next to godliness.
　　　　　　—My father

Take your own advice: if Orpheus is in it
or vultures (the impulse is the same:

skull picked clean by pain, mutilated
song, a dark hour circled, regret baring

poison-jeweled fangs) throw it out. If there
is cooking (like the one about the woman

stirring boiling polenta for two, stunned
by that volcanic hiss and bubble, its promise

that if she abandons attentiveness
the house will burn down) that becomes

a metaphor for love, throw it out. If
it is sentimental, overly lovely, throw it out.

(My guilt glows like the skin of the hornworm,
incandescent, spined, bright as the bolt

of lightning which tunes the horizon
with its silver tines.) But our darlings

are delicate cats with many lives, and I
don't buy into euthanasia. This is an age

that dies and revives. I know a single garlic
clove will live forever. I salvage and in lieu

of prayer I compost. I buy Ball jars. I root
cellar, I hoard, I shotgun. I'll bury in the yard.

A Final Study of the Anthropologist: Self-Portrait

Almost every historical atrocity has a geographically symbolic core.
——*National Geographic,* August 2012

Perhaps it is a poor place to begin (amid
pendulous breasts, the juxtaposition of the Serengeti's
tall grasses with the lion's
        eyelashes,
porous, illumined flesh that could belong

to ocean's darkness, or the body's)
but replacing *every historical atrocity* with *anything*
        we remember beyond
the moment of its passing, she
        begins to see: we seek

our place in the narrative, and so she reads
of the old heroes, whose names were carved
        into the unknown: Beowulf, Gilgamesh, Meriwether,
slayers of monsters who sent peace/cedar/live squirrels in cages

back to their cities
        and great halls. Everything worth knowing
is a story—but let it be fuller, let it be rich
as a root cellar that jars
        the memory of light. She is convinced

the new hero will draw the dark
around him like a cloak.
        He will be sedentary. He will love

blue mountains. No one has ever felt the presence of God
all the time. Let the beasts
        return. Let them speak of what they loved.

Notes and Acknowledgments

"Remains" is for Morgan Harrington.

"The Evolution of Nightmare": The old poet is Charles Wright, speaking lines from his poem "Homage to Paul Cézanne."

"Where the Sentence Ends the Sentiment Burgeons" and *"Terra Firma"* remember Blake Herman.

"Plath's Bee's": Sylvia Plath's father Otto kept bees. According to beekeeping lore, when the keeper dies someone must inform the bees. This poem borrows the line *I ordered this, this clean wood box* from Plath's poem "The Arrival of the Bee Box."

"A Study of the Anthropologist" Sections I, II, III were inspired by three professors on the University of Virginia's anthropology faculty: respectively, Roy Wagner, Ruth Danziger, and George Mentore.

"Ruin Song" responds to my experience on a small archaeological survey team among the Anasazi ruins of New Mexico's Chaco Canyon during the summer of 2008.

Section 3: George Pepper and Richard Wetherill were the leaders of the original excavations of the site, which began in 1896.

Section 9: This section was inspired by a page of *The Architecture of Chaco Canyon, New Mexico*, edited by Stephen H. Lekson.

"A Sparrow's Life's as Sweet as Mine" takes its title from John Clare's "Summer Evening."

"In Every House the Same Blue Flame" takes its title from a line in Chad Davison and Marella Feltrin-Morris' translation of Fabio Pusterla's "Star, Meteor, Some Shooting Thing."

"The Comte de Buffon Composes a Nasty Note to Thomas Jefferson Regarding His Recurring Nightmares of the American Moose": Most of my knowledge of the relationship between Georges-Louis Leclerc de Buffon (an 18th century naturalist who promoted the idea that the New World was damp, degenerate and inferior to Europe) and Thomas Jefferson (whose patriotism and love for the natural world drove him to refute the Comte) comes from Lee Alan Dugatin's book *Mr. Jefferson and the Giant Moose: Natural History in Early America.*

Grateful acknowledgement is made to the journals where these poems first appeared.

32 Poems: "My Father's Pronunciation"
The American Poetry Journal: "The Comte de Buffon Composes a Nasty Note to Thomas Jefferson Regarding His Recurring Nightmares of the American Moose"
The Carolina Quarterly: "*Scala Naturae,* or Southern Vivisection," "The Mole, the Sweet Potato, and the Possibility of Allegory"
Crab Orchard Review: "Umbrage"
Cream City Review: "Once, in College, My Father Played Horatio"
The Cumberland River Review: "*Tapetum Lucidum*"
Flyway: "Reading Charles Wright in the Desert," "Remains," "A Study of the Anthropologist I, II, III" (as a single poem), "The Whaler to His Wife," "July, and I Urge My Roots to Grow"

Fourteen Hills: "The Wisdom of Dormancy"

Fugue: "The Language of Birds"

The Journal: "Bear Hunters at McAfee's Knob"

The Mid-American Review: "While Picking Berries, I Recall the
　　Childhood Practice of Tying Junebugs to Strings, Swinging
　　Them Overhead like Balloons"

The Missouri Review Online: Poem of the Week: "Love Poem for Naming"

Perigee: "The Seed Jar"

Rattle: "Xanthus, Achilles' Immortal Warhorse, Rodeos in Amarillo"

Shenandoah: "The Evolution of Nightmare," "Leaning Toward
　　Manifesto," "Where the Sentence Ends the Sentiment Burgeons"

Smartish Pace: "Terra Firma"

The Southeast Review: "Migraine/Ecotone"

Southern Humanities Review: "Migraine/Ecotone II"

Tar River Poetry: "My Father, Digging"

Thrush: "In Every House the Same Blue Flame"

Tupelo Quarterly: "A Final Study of the Anthropologist: Self-Portrait"

Waccamaw: "A Sparrow's Life's as Sweet as Mine"

I have been given the gift of great teachers. Their wisdom, kindness, and
support have been invaluable, and this book would never have come to
be without them. I offer my sincere and humble thanks to my teachers
at the University of Virginia, including Greg Orr, Charles Wright,
Rita Dove, Sydney Blair, Adam Giannelli, and the peerless Lisa Russ
Spaar. Surely there is no greater boon for young writers than to have
their ambition and work treated with the kind of respect and attention
I found in those years.

　　I am grateful for the guidance, and the time to write and teach,
offered by the MFA Program at the University of Arkansas, as well
as the Walton Fellowship and the Writers in the Schools Program.
Thanks to John DuVal, Geoff Brock, Alexandra Teague, Skip Hayes,

and, above all, Davis McCombs: these poems could have found no better friend and advocate. Many thanks as well to my fellow writers in the program.

I thank the University of Virginia and the National Park Service for the opportunity to spend five weeks in the summer of 2008 as part of the four-person archaeological survey team in New Mexico's Chaco Culture National Historical Park.

Thanks to the readers and editors who have supported these poems with their trust and confidence. I offer particular thanks to R.T. Smith at *Shenandoah*, who continued to encourage my work long after publication with a Pushcart nomination and the 2013 James Boatwright III Prize for Poetry.

Thanks to those who helped bring this book to life, including Claudia Emerson, Pam Burnham and the Iwaski Contemporary Art Gallery, Kate Thompson, and Susan Kan and the readers at Perugia Press.

All thanks go to my parents, John and Marilee, whose support and love is everything, and every poem.

Thanks to Ben, for helping this book grow.

Thanks to Meghan, for showing the way in the dark.

About the Author

Corrie Williamson grew up on a small farm in the Shenandoah Valley of southwestern Virginia. She received her BA in Anthropology and English from the University of Virginia, and her MFA in Poetry from the University of Arkansas, where she was a Walton Fellow and Director of the Writers in the Schools Program. Her poems have recently appeared in *The Missouri Review, The Journal, The Colorado Review, Crab Orchard Review, Shenandoah,* and elsewhere.

About Perugia Press

Perugia Press publishes one collection of poetry each year, by a woman at the beginning of her publishing career. Our mission is to produce beautiful books that interest long-time readers of poetry and welcome those new to poetry. We also aim to celebrate and promote poetry whenever we can, and to keep the cultural discussion of poetry inclusive.

Also from Perugia Press:
- *Begin Empty-Handed*, Gail Martin
- *The Wishing Tomb*, Amanda Auchter
- *Gloss*, Ida Stewart
- *Each Crumbling House*, Melody S. Gee
- *How to Live on Bread and Music*, Jennifer K. Sweeney
- *Two Minutes of Light*, Nancy K. Pearson
- *Beg No Pardon*, Lynne Thompson
- *Lamb*, Frannie Lindsay
- *The Disappearing Letters*, Carol Edelstein
- *Kettle Bottom*, Diane Gilliam Fisher
- *Seamless*, Linda Tomol Pennisi
- *Red*, Melanie Braverman
- *A Wound On Stone*, Faye George
- *The Work of Hands*, Catherine Anderson
- *Reach*, Janet E. Aalfs
- *Impulse to Fly*, Almitra David
- *Finding the Bear*, Gail Thomas

This book is set in Centaur, a delicate, lyrical, and quirky type family originally designed by graphic designer Bruce Rogers in 1914. The type, first used in a version of Maurice de Guérin's *The Centaur* and named to commemorate the project, was inspired by Nicholas Jenson's 1470 Eusebius's *De praeparatione evangelica*, a watershed book in the history of printing which marks the first use of Roman-style movable type. The italics, by Frederic Warde, are based on the letterforms of sixteenth-century printer and calligrapher Ludovico degli Arrighi.